D1606499

LOG START		LOG END	

COMPANY NAME

ADDRESS

PHONE

EMAIL | **FAX**

WEB

NOTES

INDEX		
CLIENT ID	NAME	PAGE NO

CLIENT NAME		CLIENT ID

ADDRESS

PHONE NUMBER	

EMAIL	BIRTHDAY

OCCUPATION	CATEGORY ☆☆☆☆☆

DATE	TIME	SERVICE	CHARGE	NOTE

1

CLIENT NAME	CLIENT ID

ADDRESS

PHONE NUMBER	

EMAIL	BIRTHDAY

OCCUPATION	CATEGORY ☆☆☆☆☆

DATE	TIME	SERVICE	CHARGE	NOTE

NOTES

CLIENT NAME		CLIENT ID

ADDRESS

PHONE NUMBER	

EMAIL	BIRTHDAY

OCCUPATION	CATEGORY ☆☆☆☆☆

DATE	TIME	SERVICE	CHARGE	NOTE

NOTES

CLIENT NAME		CLIENT ID

ADDRESS

PHONE NUMBER	

EMAIL	BIRTHDAY

OCCUPATION	CATEGORY ☆☆☆☆☆

DATE	TIME	SERVICE	CHARGE	NOTE

NOTES

CLIENT NAME		CLIENT ID

ADDRESS

PHONE NUMBER	

EMAIL	BIRTHDAY

OCCUPATION	CATEGORY ☆☆☆☆☆

DATE	TIME	SERVICE	CHARGE	NOTE

NOTES

CLIENT NAME	CLIENT ID

ADDRESS

PHONE NUMBER	

EMAIL	BIRTHDAY

OCCUPATION	CATEGORY ☆☆☆☆☆

DATE	TIME	SERVICE	CHARGE	NOTE

NOTES

CLIENT NAME		CLIENT ID

ADDRESS

PHONE NUMBER

EMAIL	BIRTHDAY

OCCUPATION	CATEGORY ☆☆☆☆☆

DATE	TIME	SERVICE	CHARGE	NOTE

NOTES

CLIENT NAME		CLIENT ID

ADDRESS

PHONE NUMBER

EMAIL	BIRTHDAY

OCCUPATION	CATEGORY ☆☆☆☆☆

DATE	TIME	SERVICE	CHARGE	NOTE

NOTES

CLIENT NAME		CLIENT ID

ADDRESS

PHONE NUMBER

EMAIL	BIRTHDAY

OCCUPATION	CATEGORY ☆☆☆☆☆

DATE	TIME	SERVICE	CHARGE	NOTE

NOTES

CLIENT NAME		CLIENT ID

ADDRESS

PHONE NUMBER

EMAIL	BIRTHDAY

OCCUPATION	CATEGORY ☆☆☆☆☆

DATE	TIME	SERVICE	CHARGE	NOTE

NOTES

CLIENT NAME		CLIENT ID

ADDRESS

PHONE NUMBER

EMAIL	BIRTHDAY

OCCUPATION	CATEGORY ☆☆☆☆☆

DATE	TIME	SERVICE	CHARGE	NOTE

NOTES

CLIENT NAME		CLIENT ID	

ADDRESS

PHONE NUMBER

EMAIL | **BIRTHDAY**

OCCUPATION | CATEGORY ☆☆☆☆☆

DATE	TIME	SERVICE	CHARGE	NOTE

NOTES

CLIENT NAME		CLIENT ID	

ADDRESS			

PHONE NUMBER	

EMAIL	BIRTHDAY

OCCUPATION	CATEGORY ☆☆☆☆☆

DATE	TIME	SERVICE	CHARGE	NOTE

NOTES

CLIENT NAME	CLIENT ID

ADDRESS

PHONE NUMBER	

EMAIL	BIRTHDAY

OCCUPATION	CATEGORY ☆☆☆☆☆

DATE	TIME	SERVICE	CHARGE	NOTE

NOTES

CLIENT NAME		CLIENT ID	

ADDRESS

PHONE NUMBER

EMAIL	BIRTHDAY

OCCUPATION	CATEGORY ☆☆☆☆☆

DATE	TIME	SERVICE	CHARGE	NOTE

CLIENT NAME	CLIENT ID

ADDRESS

PHONE NUMBER	

EMAIL	BIRTHDAY

OCCUPATION	CATEGORY ☆☆☆☆☆

DATE	TIME	SERVICE	CHARGE	NOTE

CLIENT NAME	CLIENT ID

ADDRESS

PHONE NUMBER	

EMAIL	BIRTHDAY

OCCUPATION	CATEGORY ☆☆☆☆☆

DATE	TIME	SERVICE	CHARGE	NOTE

NOTES

CLIENT NAME		CLIENT ID

ADDRESS

PHONE NUMBER	

EMAIL	BIRTHDAY

OCCUPATION	CATEGORY ☆☆☆☆☆

DATE	TIME	SERVICE	CHARGE	NOTE

NOTES

CLIENT NAME		CLIENT ID

ADDRESS

PHONE NUMBER

EMAIL	BIRTHDAY

OCCUPATION	CATEGORY ☆☆☆☆☆

DATE	TIME	SERVICE	CHARGE	NOTE

NOTES

CLIENT NAME		CLIENT ID

ADDRESS

PHONE NUMBER	

EMAIL	BIRTHDAY

OCCUPATION	CATEGORY ☆☆☆☆☆

DATE	TIME	SERVICE	CHARGE	NOTE

NOTES

CLIENT NAME		CLIENT ID

ADDRESS

PHONE NUMBER	

EMAIL	BIRTHDAY

OCCUPATION	CATEGORY ☆☆☆☆☆

DATE	TIME	SERVICE	CHARGE	NOTE

NOTES

CLIENT NAME	CLIENT ID

ADDRESS

PHONE NUMBER	

EMAIL	BIRTHDAY

OCCUPATION	CATEGORY ☆☆☆☆☆

DATE	TIME	SERVICE	CHARGE	NOTE

NOTES

	CLIENT NAME		CLIENT ID	

ADDRESS		

PHONE NUMBER	

EMAIL	BIRTHDAY

OCCUPATION	CATEGORY ☆☆☆☆☆

DATE	TIME	SERVICE	CHARGE	NOTE

NOTES

CLIENT NAME	CLIENT ID

ADDRESS

PHONE NUMBER	

EMAIL	BIRTHDAY

OCCUPATION	CATEGORY ☆☆☆☆☆

DATE	TIME	SERVICE	CHARGE	NOTE

NOTES

CLIENT NAME	CLIENT ID

ADDRESS

PHONE NUMBER	

EMAIL	BIRTHDAY

OCCUPATION	CATEGORY ☆☆☆☆☆

DATE	TIME	SERVICE	CHARGE	NOTE

NOTES

CLIENT NAME			CLIENT ID	

ADDRESS

PHONE NUMBER

EMAIL | BIRTHDAY

OCCUPATION | CATEGORY ☆☆☆☆☆

DATE	TIME	SERVICE	CHARGE	NOTE

NOTES

CLIENT NAME			CLIENT ID	

ADDRESS

PHONE NUMBER

EMAIL		BIRTHDAY	

OCCUPATION		CATEGORY ☆☆☆☆☆	

DATE	TIME	SERVICE	CHARGE	NOTE

NOTES

CLIENT NAME		CLIENT ID

ADDRESS

PHONE NUMBER	

EMAIL	BIRTHDAY

OCCUPATION	CATEGORY ☆☆☆☆☆

DATE	TIME	SERVICE	CHARGE	NOTE

NOTES

CLIENT NAME		CLIENT ID

ADDRESS

PHONE NUMBER

EMAIL

BIRTHDAY

OCCUPATION

CATEGORY ☆☆☆☆☆

DATE	TIME	SERVICE	CHARGE	NOTE

57

NOTES

CLIENT NAME		CLIENT ID

ADDRESS

PHONE NUMBER

EMAIL | BIRTHDAY

OCCUPATION | CATEGORY ☆☆☆☆☆

DATE	TIME	SERVICE	CHARGE	NOTE

CLIENT NAME		CLIENT ID

ADDRESS

PHONE NUMBER	

EMAIL	BIRTHDAY

OCCUPATION	CATEGORY ☆☆☆☆☆

DATE	TIME	SERVICE	CHARGE	NOTE

61

NOTES

CLIENT NAME	CLIENT ID

ADDRESS

PHONE NUMBER	

EMAIL	BIRTHDAY

OCCUPATION	CATEGORY ☆☆☆☆☆

DATE	TIME	SERVICE	CHARGE	NOTE

CLIENT NAME		CLIENT ID

ADDRESS

PHONE NUMBER	

EMAIL	BIRTHDAY

OCCUPATION	CATEGORY ☆☆☆☆☆

DATE	TIME	SERVICE	CHARGE	NOTE

CLIENT NAME		CLIENT ID

ADDRESS

PHONE NUMBER	

EMAIL	BIRTHDAY

OCCUPATION	CATEGORY ☆☆☆☆☆

DATE	TIME	SERVICE	CHARGE	NOTE

NOTES

CLIENT NAME			CLIENT ID	

ADDRESS

PHONE NUMBER

EMAIL | **BIRTHDAY**

OCCUPATION | CATEGORY ☆☆☆☆☆

DATE	TIME	SERVICE	CHARGE	NOTE

| CLIENT NAME | CLIENT ID |

ADDRESS

| PHONE NUMBER | |

| EMAIL | BIRTHDAY |

| OCCUPATION | CATEGORY ☆☆☆☆☆ |

DATE	TIME	SERVICE	CHARGE	NOTE

| CLIENT NAME | CLIENT ID |

| ADDRESS |

| PHONE NUMBER | |

| EMAIL | BIRTHDAY |

| OCCUPATION | CATEGORY ☆☆☆☆☆ |

DATE	TIME	SERVICE	CHARGE	NOTE

NOTES

CLIENT NAME	CLIENT ID

ADDRESS

PHONE NUMBER	

EMAIL	BIRTHDAY

OCCUPATION	CATEGORY ☆☆☆☆☆

DATE	TIME	SERVICE	CHARGE	NOTE

NOTES

CLIENT NAME		CLIENT ID		

ADDRESS

PHONE NUMBER

EMAIL	BIRTHDAY

OCCUPATION	CATEGORY ☆☆☆☆☆

DATE	TIME	SERVICE	CHARGE	NOTE

77

NOTES

CLIENT NAME		CLIENT ID

ADDRESS

PHONE NUMBER |

EMAIL	BIRTHDAY

OCCUPATION | CATEGORY ☆☆☆☆☆

DATE	TIME	SERVICE	CHARGE	NOTE

NOTES

CLIENT NAME		CLIENT ID

ADDRESS

PHONE NUMBER

EMAIL	BIRTHDAY

OCCUPATION	CATEGORY ☆☆☆☆☆

DATE	TIME	SERVICE	CHARGE	NOTE

CLIENT NAME			CLIENT ID	

ADDRESS

PHONE NUMBER	

EMAIL	BIRTHDAY

OCCUPATION	CATEGORY ☆☆☆☆☆

DATE	TIME	SERVICE	CHARGE	NOTE

NOTES

CLIENT NAME	CLIENT ID

ADDRESS

PHONE NUMBER	

EMAIL	BIRTHDAY

OCCUPATION	CATEGORY ☆☆☆☆☆

DATE	TIME	SERVICE	CHARGE	NOTE

NOTES

| CLIENT NAME | CLIENT ID |

ADDRESS

PHONE NUMBER

EMAIL | BIRTHDAY

OCCUPATION | CATEGORY ☆☆☆☆☆

DATE	TIME	SERVICE	CHARGE	NOTE

NOTES

CLIENT NAME		CLIENT ID

ADDRESS

PHONE NUMBER	

EMAIL	BIRTHDAY

OCCUPATION	CATEGORY ☆☆☆☆☆

DATE	TIME	SERVICE	CHARGE	NOTE

NOTES

CLIENT NAME		CLIENT ID

ADDRESS

PHONE NUMBER	

EMAIL	BIRTHDAY

OCCUPATION	CATEGORY ☆☆☆☆☆

DATE	TIME	SERVICE	CHARGE	NOTE

CLIENT NAME		CLIENT ID

ADDRESS

PHONE NUMBER	

EMAIL	BIRTHDAY

OCCUPATION	CATEGORY ☆☆☆☆☆

DATE	TIME	SERVICE	CHARGE	NOTE

	CLIENT NAME			CLIENT ID	

ADDRESS	

	PHONE NUMBER	

	EMAIL		BIRTHDAY

	OCCUPATION	CATEGORY ☆☆☆☆☆

DATE	TIME	SERVICE	CHARGE	NOTE

CLIENT NAME		CLIENT ID	

ADDRESS

PHONE NUMBER

EMAIL	BIRTHDAY

OCCUPATION	CATEGORY ☆☆☆☆☆

DATE	TIME	SERVICE	CHARGE	NOTE

CLIENT NAME		CLIENT ID

ADDRESS

PHONE NUMBER

EMAIL	BIRTHDAY

OCCUPATION	CATEGORY ☆☆☆☆☆

DATE	TIME	SERVICE	CHARGE	NOTE

NOTES

100

CLIENT NAME		CLIENT ID

ADDRESS

PHONE NUMBER	

EMAIL	BIRTHDAY

OCCUPATION	CATEGORY ☆☆☆☆☆

DATE	TIME	SERVICE	CHARGE	NOTE

CLIENT NAME		CLIENT ID

ADDRESS

PHONE NUMBER	

EMAIL	BIRTHDAY

OCCUPATION	CATEGORY ☆☆☆☆☆

DATE	TIME	SERVICE	CHARGE	NOTE

CLIENT NAME	CLIENT ID

ADDRESS

PHONE NUMBER

EMAIL	BIRTHDAY

OCCUPATION	CATEGORY ☆☆☆☆☆

DATE	TIME	SERVICE	CHARGE	NOTE

CLIENT NAME		CLIENT ID

ADDRESS

PHONE NUMBER	

EMAIL	BIRTHDAY

OCCUPATION	CATEGORY ☆☆☆☆☆

DATE	TIME	SERVICE	CHARGE	NOTE

CLIENT NAME		CLIENT ID

ADDRESS

PHONE NUMBER	

EMAIL	BIRTHDAY

OCCUPATION	CATEGORY ☆☆☆☆☆

DATE	TIME	SERVICE	CHARGE	NOTE

CLIENT NAME		CLIENT ID

ADDRESS

PHONE NUMBER	

EMAIL	BIRTHDAY

OCCUPATION	CATEGORY ☆☆☆☆☆

DATE	TIME	SERVICE	CHARGE	NOTE

CLIENT NAME		CLIENT ID

ADDRESS

PHONE NUMBER

EMAIL	BIRTHDAY

OCCUPATION	CATEGORY ☆☆☆☆☆

DATE	TIME	SERVICE	CHARGE	NOTE

CLIENT NAME		CLIENT ID

ADDRESS

PHONE NUMBER	

EMAIL	BIRTHDAY

OCCUPATION	CATEGORY ☆☆☆☆☆

DATE	TIME	SERVICE	CHARGE	NOTE

NOTES

CLIENT NAME		CLIENT ID

ADDRESS

PHONE NUMBER	

EMAIL	BIRTHDAY

OCCUPATION	CATEGORY ☆☆☆☆☆

DATE	TIME	SERVICE	CHARGE	NOTE